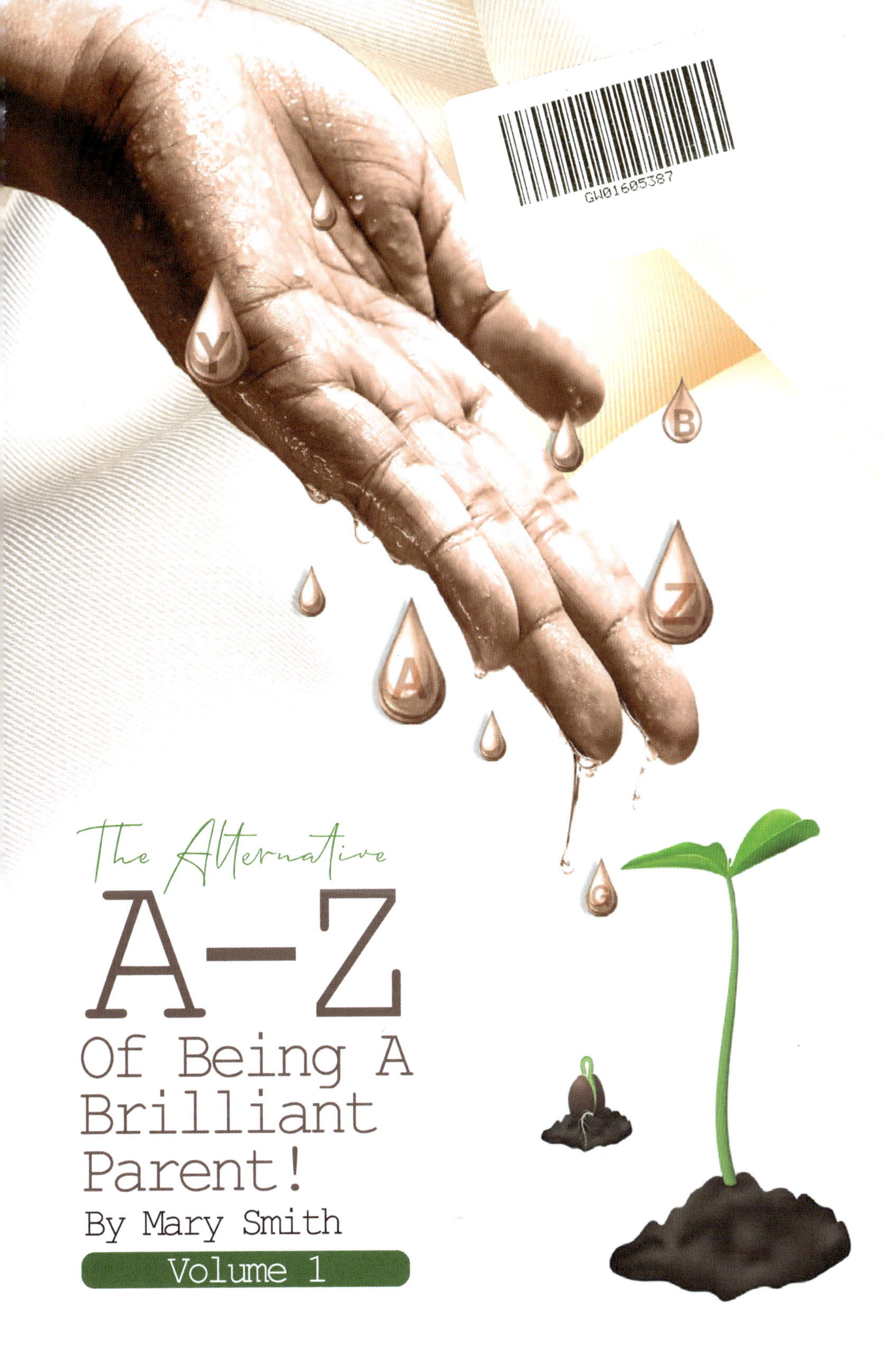

The Alternative

A-Z

Of Being A Brilliant Parent!

By Mary Smith

Volume 1

This book is dedicated to my mother, Augustine Smith, who, although not having received a formal education, followed her intuition and single-handedly raised three successful children. I also dedicate this book to those parents who, despite not understanding the parenting job description they signed-up to, are trying their best with the knowledge and resources they have, to raise healthy, well-adjusted children who can positively contribute to the world.

This book provides parents with the opportunity to step back from the business of parenting and step into...being a Brilliant Parent!

M. Smith

About the Author

Mary is the Principal of social enterprise, *Brilliant Parents*, which seeks to transform the parenting skills of the nation. Through her practice as a parent support practitioner, Mary has been advising and supporting thousands of parents and their families for over 10 years.

Mary is regarded as 'a thought leader on parental relations and development' and her mission is to facilitate the enrichment and quality of the parent-child relationship, improve child outcomes through positive parenting and transform the life trajectory of children through civil society.

Her work is a direct by-product of her own experiences as a mother. Mary considers these experiences to be her 'on-the-job' training and pivotal to her professional mandate.

Thank you

It would be remiss of me not to thank the organisation *Brilliant Parents* and my board of Directors, Angela Barst, Desiree Mahoney and Yvonne Robinson and my Course Manager, Annmarie Fevrier who have all enabled me to make my vision a reality. With their support we have literally impacted thousands of parents through the vital work of the organisation.

AUTHOR

Contents

About the Book

Parenting is one of life's special privileges. However, the complexity of parenting, and its related dynamics, is often unfairly examined. Difficulties within the parent-child dynamic are often attributed to a problem rooted within the child. Society then projects this message. Parents are rarely encouraged to self-reflect and seldom signposted to the resources that can offer beneficial support and self-help. Therefore, parents need all the help they can get!

The Alternative A-Z of Being a Brilliant Parent! meets this need by being your personal guide and self-help book that provides you - the parent - with an opportunity to pause, recall and honestly reflect upon your own behaviour and its roots. This also give you time to examine whether you would like to change aspects of your own parenting style, prior to re-engaging with your child.

By exploring an array of parenting subjects such as 'boundaries' and 'influence', and those that are less obvious, including 'environment' and 'pruning', this book will support you.

Foreword

The Alternative A-Z of Being a Brilliant Parent!

Anyone can have a child, but it takes more than simply having a child to be a good parent to that child....

The relationship that a parent has with a child (irrespective of whether that parent is biological or non-biological) is not only at the core of the dynamics of a family unit, but it is one of the principal tenets upon which a community or indeed, a whole society functions. Once an individual becomes a parent, it is a role that, in theory, should exist for a lifetime, but sadly for some parents, the mere thought of parental responsibility per se, let alone being wedded to the idea of lifetime parental responsibility, is an abhorrent one.

Notwithstanding such a sobering thought, the relationship that a parent has with his/her child is not only crucial to the physical and emotional development of that child, it also serves as the defining platform for the character of that child when he/she assumes adulthood. This will, in turn, define and influence any future relationship with any offspring that the child themselves may have.

Parenting abilities and skills do not remain constant. They evolve from generation to generation as well as differ from culture to culture but the one thing that all parents throughout the differing generations and cultures have in common, is their aim to achieve the ideal of being a good, or indeed, a brilliant parent. But what makes a good/brilliant parent? "One man's brilliant parent, may be another man's bad tyrant...." and I suppose the best way to help attain the nirvana of good/brilliant parenting skills is presumably, the ability to recognise bad parenting practice and to try as best as you can to improve on any parenting skill deficiencies.

There may be some truth in the argument that the goal of being a good/brilliant parent is by its very definition, simply unattainable. That supposition may indeed be true, but this A-Z guide of being a brilliant parent is a long way along the road towards achieving that aim without making any outlandish claim that it actually does!

I have been a Patron of *Brilliant Parents* since 2018, an organisation that I feel both honoured and privileged to have my name associated with. An organisation that, I have no doubt, will continue to grow and expand and provide a crucial platform for good parenting skills and practice.

Dr Shaun Wallace

Introduction

A parenting role may be undertaken by a biological parent, a carer or through other guardianship roles. Accordingly, use of the word, 'parent' in this book applies to anyone who is responsible for another human being who is younger in age.

Expectant parents generally feel acquainted with the parenting job description at the start of the parenting journey. However, quite often, it is not until one takes on the role that reality sets in. Parenting is a role unlike any other. There is no remuneration for parenting and not much thanks either. However, it is a job that many of us sign-up to, time and time again, despite its financial, physical and emotional costs.

The Alternative A-Z of Being a Brilliant Parent! addresses many 'under-the-surface' characteristics and dynamics of parenting. This book is for all parents, including those who, like me, felt they were equipped to do the job, only to realise over time that they were neither fortified with the skills to parent confidently, nor armed with the know-how to parent competently and as a result, had to learn quickly. In fact, for some of us, much of our own childhood experiences left us with so little self-esteem, that consequently, there was a lack of understanding on how to healthily meet our needs, whilst meeting the necessities and demands of a child, in order that they may flourish.

This book will also support parents who self-identify as having competent parenting skills, but who wish to undertake a self-inventory on those less-obvious parenting characteristics, to ensure they have covered all the bases and where needed, to upgrade their parenting skills.

I have drawn on my personal experience as a daughter and mother and from the years spent training parents in the key components of positive parenting, the outcome of which you may find beneficial for your *Brilliant Parents* Toolbox. I commend all parents for taking the time to step back from the business of parenting, in order to step into working 'on' the business of parenting and to being open to receiving an alternative perspective that will support the development of a new parenting skill set.

For those of you, who, for far too long have called yourself a bad mum or dad and feel you are failing in your parenting skills, the good news is that parenting is a modifiable skill. Therefore, my prayer for you, is that, as a result of understanding and implementing components of this book, you will not judge yourself too harshly.

I liken parenting a child to nurturing a plant. Those of us new to gardening may have to research how to go about getting the best out of our plants and similarly, I have come to understand that it should also be the case with parenting. Fortunately, most parents, by default, end up raising mature, healthy children who become emotionally sound young adults, who then go on to blossom and contribute positively to the world. However sometimes, like plants, despite our best efforts, our child may not flower in the way we expected, or our child's personality may have been affected by what they experienced in their 'childhood nursery' and even with the best will in the world, our growing plant may not respond to our chosen method of nurturing, after all not all plants like the sun!

The Alternative A-Z of Being a Brilliant Parent! will give you an opportunity to focus on the key ingredients you need to add to your relationship with your growing child so that you can look back and feel confident that you tried your best with the knowledge and resources you had at the time, whether they be your children, grandchildren, step-children, adopted children or foster children; all children will benefit from your efforts to become a brilliant parent!

“A” for Assertive

How many of us can honestly say that we are assertive? Do you tend to veer on the passive or the aggressive side? Whichever style you relate to naturally, will tend to be the way you parent. Imagine you are driving along, and another driver comes from nowhere and cuts you up. Do you say calmly, bless you and wish them well or do you use some choice words instead? Either way, whatever your child observes when you face conflict, they are likely to replicate!

Assertiveness does not always come naturally to us unless we work at it. Part of being assertive when being a parent, is to remain calm, follow through and keep to our word.

Being assertive takes strength. The easiest thing to do for most parents is to react. Animals react! If you pull a dog's tail it is likely to snarl back at you and maybe even bite you. We human beings have been given the luxury of being able to process behaviour and choose whether to react immediately or respond after giving the situation some thought.

To be an assertive parent is not to be a soft touch, but rather to communicate calmly through our words and deeds what is acceptable and what is not and to act on both, whether that be through rewards or consequences.

Therefore, my gift to you is to consider the following statements and questions:

- What type of parents were your parents - assertive, passive, or aggressive?
- Which of the above styles have you adopted?
- What single thing could you do to become more assertive in your parenting?
- How do you think this change might affect your child's behaviour?

"B" for Boundaries

How many of you find it easy to put boundaries in place with regards to what you will and will not accept from your children? How many of you know what your non-negotiables are?

Boundaries are a necessary part of all our lives. However, some of us find it difficult to give our children that essential vitamin and I do not mean vitamin B or C, but Vitamin NO. Why is that? Do we hate confrontation, do we want our children to have what we didn't have as we were growing up, or are we trying to over-compensate for a mother or father that is no longer in our child's life?

Either way, think about what you are teaching your child every time you ignore a misbehaviour. Are you really helping them? It might appear that way in the short term, but what will your child look like in ten years' time when they do not have the capacity to accept the word "no" or do not understand when they have over-stepped the mark? Boundaries are a necessary requirement of life. By saying NO, you are teaching your child that they cannot have everything they want in life, which for some children can be a bitter pill to swallow, if not given regularly!

Therefore, my gift to you is to consider the following statements and questions:

- Identify what is a non-negotiable that your child understands.
- Remember when the last time was that you told your child no.
- Examine how your child typically responds when told no.
- Decide whether your boundaries are not being adhered to because you are not following through.

“C” for Change

Do you have the courage to change your own behaviour and as a result, that of your child's? Over 95% of parents who seek support, do so because they want to improve some aspect of their child's behaviour, whether it be their child's general attitude, too much screen time, or not doing their homework. The funny thing is, we parents very rarely look at ourselves! Instead, we inadvertently create a dance which looks something like this:

The child misbehaves, the parent then requests that their behaviour is changed but the child ignores the request, so the request gets louder and louder and only when the parent is about to burst a gasket does the child listen!

Parents say to me, but he/she will not listen unless I shout, and they wonder who taught their child the dance! A 'waltz' or a 'tango' requires a lead dancer, so too do our children. We, the parents, are the lead and as such, we decide the steps, the timing, and the change of direction. Maybe it is time to change the steps.

If you can find the courage to change the dance - you are more likely to change your child's behaviour!

Therefore, my gift to you is to consider the following statements and questions:

- Identify when the last time was that you had to confront a big change in your life.
- Understand how well you adjusted to that change.
- Consider whether your attitude to change is mirrored by your child.
- Decide whether you are ready to do the work to change certain aspects of your own behaviour.

"D" for Decisive

How many of us start off responding to our child's request with a strong 'No', only to change our minds minutes later with a reluctant 'Yes' after our child has had a meltdown in public or just got on our nerves? Each time you change your mind, think, what are you teaching your child?

Our children know our strengths and our weaknesses. They will know when we are feeling challenged, in what situations and in front of which members of our family or friends. Therefore, if you wish to be an assertive parent, you will need to be a decisive parent, whereby your 'Yes' means 'Yes' and your 'No' means 'No'. Sometimes you may need some 'wriggle room' as I call it and a 'we'll see', or 'I will let you know', may be appropriate.

Sometimes, one parent might be more decisive than the other and your child will know instinctively, which is which. The question is, which parent does your child listen to, first time? Chances are, it is the one who is more decisive!

Therefore, my gift to you is to consider the following statements and questions:

- Identify when the last time was that you changed your mind because of your child's misbehaviour.
- How does your child react when you are being decisive?
- Understand the long-term benefits to your child of your being decisive.
- Commit to keeping to your decisions, regardless of your child's possible protests.

"E" for Environment

A child's environment is created by its parents, physically, emotionally and spiritually. You sometimes hear grown adults reminisce about growing up in poverty, but despite this, experiencing an extremely happy childhood! Money, or having the latest gadget, does not create long-term happiness from a child's point of view but knowing that they are loved and valued is sufficient. Children who grow up in a negative environment or experience not feeling valued, can go on to accept that as the norm when becoming adults.

The home is your child's primary school and therefore you are their primary teacher! Therefore, what is your primary school like? What kind of relationship do you, their primary teacher, have with your child? Are you nurturing, loving, patient and happy or are you always arguing, shouting at your partner and feeling unhappy most of the time? What is your child exposed to? Whichever it is, whether your home is happy or sad, the effects can make an indelible mark on your child.

So, consider your child's current environment and like your plants, consider whether you need to move their position slightly to encourage nourishment and thriving. Plants, like children, flourish in the right environment when they both receive the right quantity of light, water, and love.

Therefore, my gift to you is to consider the following statements and questions:

- What kind of environment is your child growing up in?
- Do you need to change your physical home environment in some way, if so, in what way?
- Is your own behaviour affecting your child's environment?
- Make a commitment to ensuring that your child's environment is conducive to peace and love.

"F" for Focus

How well do you focus? What kinds of things do you focus on? Imagine, your teenager decides to clean their room. You see it, but you say nothing, instead you think, well she knows what I expect. The following day you find dirty cups in her room and at that point you call her by her name, tell her that is not acceptable and remind her of the rules.

Most of us parents have, at some time, ignored our children's behaviour when they are behaving well, but the minute they start to play up, we do not even have to see it, we can smell misbehaviour a mile off and it is at that point that they have our full attention.

The funny thing is, did you know that whatever we focus on expands? So, if we want more of that good behaviour try looking for it, you never know, you might be surprised at what you see!

Therefore, my gift to you is to consider the following statements and questions:

- Identify whether you tend to focus on your child's negative behaviour.
- Monitor one day in your child's life to observe their behaviour.
- Commit to focusing on your child's positive behaviour each day.
- Monitor any changes in your behaviour once you start to notice more of your child's positive behaviour.

"G" for Growth

Did you know that our children are our greatest teachers and some of the biggest lessons we will learn in life are courtesy of them? This is particularly true whenever you feel emotionally charged by something your child has done. Rather than look for the answer externally and blame your child, it might be time to look within.

It could be that you hate being disrespected. Is there something about being disrespected that triggers your emotions? Was this something you felt as a child when spoken to by your parents or your siblings? Do you feel you were never taken seriously, or were you bullied whilst at school?

The sad thing is that, unless some of us can stop looking at our child as the main cause of many of our problems and asking what is wrong with them, things will never change. Maybe, just maybe it is time to focus on our own self-growth and ask, is there something wrong with me?

Therefore, my gift to you is to consider the following statements and questions:

- Identify whether you carry with you some childhood issues, which have not yet been resolved.
- Understand that these issues may be having a detrimental impact on your parenting.
- Commit to noticing when your reactions have more to do with your own unresolved issues than your child's behaviour.
- Pledge to investigate those issues, perhaps by talking to a family member, friend, GP or a counsellor.

"H" for Help

Some people find it difficult to ask for help as they consider it a weakness; sometimes letting their pride get in the way. The African proverb: it takes a village to raise a child, recognises that raising children is no mean feat. It is rewarding and fulfilling, but it can also be challenging and demanding.

Most of us parent the way we were parented and if we were lucky, we had good parents who loved and disciplined us in equal measure. It is not uncommon as parents, to call on family members and friends to help with childcare, for instance.

So why do we find it so hard to rely on these same family and friends for advice when our children are misbehaving? Is it the judgement we fear, or the failure we feel as a parent? Either way, consider that asking for help takes strength of character and is not a weakness.

Therefore, my gift to you is to consider the following statements and questions:

- Identify whether you prefer to keep your parenting concerns private because of pride.
- Clarify why this might be the case.
- Identify a trusted friend or family member to share your concerns with.
- Share your problem and or find professional help if needs be.

"I" for Inner-child

Did you know that, as adults, each of us carries with us, our inner-child? Your inner-child remembers all the scars and experiences of your childhood and, as a result, can sometimes still react like a child, both positively and negatively.

On the plus side, many of us need to tap into our inner-child and at times, not take life too seriously, remembering to laugh more and be more playful and spontaneous, particularly with our children. However, some adults received too little or not enough attention as children and have then gone on to become parents who have not healed from childhood trauma or negative experiences and consequently, may not have learned to take responsibility for their actions or learned to empathise. They may have used manipulation as a way to get what they wanted from their own parents and now, sadly, they do not have the awareness or capacity to change.

Like a child who has a tantrum, a parent's inner-child can do likewise, and this tantrum can also manifest itself in childish behaviour and have a detrimental effect on our children. Apart from not being able to set a good example, it can leave the child feeling confused and that nothing they do is right!

As such, take the time to address your inner-child, you may be surprised at what you find!

Therefore, my gift to you is to consider the following statements and questions:

- Have you heard the term inner-child?
- Are you ready to parent your inner-child?
- Can you see how your inner-child has impacted your parenting?
- What areas of your inner-child need nurturing?

"J" for Judgement

Have you ever felt judged? Have you ever judged another? Of course you have, we all have. The saying 'never judge a book by its cover' is undeniably true, but despite this, many of us fall foul and do not hesitate to reach our own negative conclusions.

Parents often tell me that they feel judged by their family or friends. Feeling judged, particularly from those people whom you would hope would be your ally, can cause immense pain.

Sometimes, those who are quick to judge, do so because either they:

- Have their own insecurity issues;
- May be jealous;
- Lack compassion because their children may be well behaved;
- Have unknowingly been manipulated by others to misjudge you, or it could be that they do not know the true context.

If you find yourself and your children being judged by friends and family or indeed by complete strangers, remember that their judgement does not have to define who you are!

Therefore, my gift to you is to consider the following statements and questions:

- Commit to not taking other people's judgement personally.
- Notice when you are judging others unfairly.
- Refrain from judging your own child harshly.
- Dedicate yourself to looking beyond the surface regarding your child's behaviour.

"K" for Knowledge

It is often said that you do not know what you do not know and that is so true. So many of us become parents, really having no idea what lies ahead of us. Parenting is one of the most demanding jobs there is. To be a parent is to be a manager, counsellor, coach, teacher, trainer, mentor, chef, housekeeper etc. Most managers have training, so why not have training for parents. The fact is, most parents learn through trial and error, but it does not have to be that way.

Any manager who wants to be the best they can be, will consider enrolling on some kind of training, and therefore it stands to reason that parenting, which I would argue is a 24/7 role, requires even more training.

If you want to increase your knowledge base when it comes to parenting, check out the books, videos and parenting courses available. After all, knowledge really is power.

Therefore, my gift to you is to consider the following statements and questions:

- Apologise if and when you have mismanaged your child's misbehaviour, due to a lack of knowledge on how best to respond.
- Discuss any concerns with your child's school to ascertain whether you can work together to improve certain behaviours pertaining to your child.
- Read pertinent books or watch relevant videos on parenting.
- Commit to lifelong learning regarding positive parenting.

“L” for Love

Our children need both love and discipline. That combination creates a healthy well-adjusted child. But how much do you love yourself, how self-disciplined are you as a parent? You cannot give what you have not got! Some parents struggle to show love, largely because they perhaps did not receive it themselves. A child without their parent's love is like a flower without sustenance, and struggles emotionally, often looking to new horizons in order to feel loved.

Alternatively, a child who feels loved, develops healthy self-esteem and confidence. So, if you want to increase your child's self-love, consider your child's understanding of love.

Sometimes the love we show our child is not received in the way we would have liked. As a parent, it is important that we acknowledge and understand our child's 'love language', which is distinctive to every individual. As such, we may feel we are doing our best, but your child may prefer to know that they are loved in one of the following five ways: to be told that they are loved, to receive gifts, to be hugged, to have you do something for them or to spend time with you.

Understanding what they best respond to, takes time. It requires observation to understand what the best 'compost' is, that your child will respond to. When you show your child that you hold them in high esteem, they are more likely to develop their own capacity to love themselves and others.

Therefore, my gift to you is to consider the following statements and questions:

- Identify how you personally like to receive love.
- Share this with your child and ask how they prefer to receive love.
- Try to express your love daily to your child.
- Undertake to take your child's preferred method of receiving love into consideration.

'The 5 Love Languages: The Secret to Love That Lasts by Gary Chapman'

"M" for Monitoring

Do you think you can accurately guess how often your child responds with a 'please' and a 'thank you' in a week? Do you think you can guess how often they disobey you in a week? The truth is, if we really want to know how often a behaviour is happening, we need to monitor that behaviour.

However, before you monitor your child, it might be interesting for you, the parent, to consider monitoring your own behaviour! How often do you read a book with your toddler, watch a film with your teenager, or perhaps just simply remain calm when your child does something you perceive as upsetting? Once you have the answer, you can then set about making any necessary changes.

When a behaviour is monitored, it gives you the ability to see either stagnation or improvement, the fiction, or the facts. You decide.

Therefore, my gift to you is to consider the following statements and questions:

- Have you ever monitored your own behaviour?
- Choose one behaviour of your own and monitor this over the next week.
- Once monitored, if you saw something you would like to change, do you have the courage to take action?
- Observe whether your family members notice the change.

"N" for Nurture

What kind of things can you do as a parent to nurture your child? Do you know what to expect from your children at different stages in their development? Do you know whether they have any additional needs? If not, you may misinterpret their behaviour and think they are being belligerent when that is not the case and therefore you do not nurture them in the way that they need. They may need support to manage their emotions when upset, they may need support to process information or they may just need extra reassurance.

Our children need to know that we see them, that they matter to us and are worthy of our love. We nurture them by respecting, accepting and loving them simply for who they are, warts and all!

So, shower your children with love, tend to their roots to make sure that their petals are full of colour. In doing so, by shining your light on them, they will learn how to navigate their way through life with respect, empathy, consideration and love for themselves and mankind.

Therefore, my gift to you is to consider the following statements and questions:

- Do you take time out for yourself?
- Consider how you can nurture yourself.
- Choose one way of nurturing yourself to put into practice this week.
- Choose one new way of nurturing your child this week.

"O" for Over-Compensation

When parents experience feelings of guilt, they can often over-compensate to make themselves feel better. However, quite often they do not take the time to think about the effects this over-compensation may have on their child.

Sometimes, parents over-compensate because there is conflict at home, or because they may have separated from their partner. Other times, it may be because parents do not spend a lot of time with their child.

Over-compensation can manifest itself in many forms, it may be an overload of gifts, allowing your child to eat whatever they want, when they want, it may be that you let them go to bed at any time or you let your teenager stay out with friends indefinitely.

The problem is that sometimes, going the extra mile when you cannot afford to, particularly financially, to meet a child's endless demands, does them no favours. This can also lead to a gradual sense of entitlement and the demise of any possibility of gratitude.

Therefore, my gift to you is to consider the following statements and questions:

- Do you feel that you have ever over-compensated with your child?
- If so, do you know why?
- How has this over-compensation manifested itself?
- Did it have the desired effect with your child?

"P" for Pruning

Most gardeners recommend that you regularly prune your plants in order to get rid of disease and to shape the plant, so it doesn't grow outside of its designated space and so it is with children. As parents, we need to know when to be patient and ignore certain minor behaviours, but there are other times when it may be necessary to prune our children's behaviour, so they do not come out of their lane, as it were.

If you want your child to bear much fruit in the long term, it might be that you must remind them at times that you are their parent and as such, certain issues are not of their concern. For example, whilst having a private telephone conversation, your child may ask you, "who you are talking to?".

Pruning takes courage and is not often met with thanks, but it does clearly illustrate to your child that you have certain expectations. Without pruning, your child is just growing; with regular pruning they will grow into a shape that embodies respect for themselves and others.

Therefore, my gift to you is to consider the following statements and questions:

- When did you last have to remind your child of an unacceptable behaviour?
- Do you have the courage to prune?
- Are you fair with your pruning, or do you sometimes go overboard?
- Do you need to do more regular pruning of your child's behaviours?

"Q" for Question

Questions, questions, questions. When it comes to our children, asking questions, serves more than one purpose. It enables them to broaden their imagination and curiosity; it enables us, the parent, to understand who they are and their thought processes; and helps to forge conversations between the parent and child, thus strengthening the relationship.

Questions can be a useful tool for toddlers, right through to young adults, to build and nourish your relationship with your child. If we want to keep our children's minds open, asking questions is a good place to start.

So, consider moving beyond the typical, 'how was your day?' question and ask more creative questions. For younger children, perhaps simply ask, 'what makes you happy?'. For older children, consider asking, 'what are three things you would like to do in your next school holiday?'.

Ask questions, do not assume, you may be surprised by what you hear.

Therefore, my gift to you is to consider the following statements and questions:

- Demonstrate your interest in your child by asking questions.
- Encourage your child to be curious and ask questions.
- Use questions to keep a discussion going.
- If you are trying to find out the motive behind a behaviour, ask questions.

"R" for Reflection

All parents make mistakes from time to time in terms of how they exhibit their parenting skills. Most of us parent the way we were parented, which could be good, bad, or somewhere in the middle. Some parents know instinctively the right way to parent and even then, they too make mistakes.

Conflict between parent and child is often at a time when our parenting skills are put to the test and sometimes, we do not manage this conflict in a fair or rational way, which can lead to resentment on both sides. It is at these times when reflection is needed. Regular reflection after every engagement is a vital part of parenting if we are to improve our parenting skills - whether the engagement is good or bad.

Give yourself a pat on the back when you have improved and cut yourself some slack and commit to doing better next time, when you slip up. After all, you are only human.

Therefore, my gift to you is to consider the following statements and questions:

- Do you have the capacity to self-reflect on your own behaviour or are you always right?
- When was the last time you reflected and took responsibility for your actions?
- Do you encourage your child to self-reflect?
- Do you consider those that can self-reflect an indication of maturity or not?

"S" for Self-Discipline

As parents, many of us feel it is our responsibility to control our children's behaviour, but as parents, how good are we at controlling our own behaviour? Self-discipline speaks volumes. Generally, we expect our children to listen, to obey, to do their homework, etc. However, sometimes, as parents, we struggle to control ourselves.

Some of us struggle with our own self-discipline when it comes to remaining calm when upset with our children, some of us struggle to lose weight, give up smoking, exercise regularly, or eat healthily, but yet we still expect our children to have the self-discipline to do what we want them to do.

Self-discipline is the ability to control and work hard or behave in a particular way, independently. So, the next time your child fails to exercise their self-discipline, it might be time to remember how difficult it can be to develop your own self-discipline 'muscle'.

Therefore, my gift to you is to consider the following statements and questions:

- Do you consider yourself to be a disciplined person?
- Are there areas in your life where you feel you could be more disciplined?
- Can you remember a time when you remained calm, instead of arguing?
- Commit to focusing on one area to exercise self-discipline in your life.

"T" for Thinking-errors

The ability to think is one of the blessings of being a human being. However, what kinds of conversation do you have with yourself regarding how you see yourself and others, in particular, your children?

Do your thoughts help or hinder your parenting? Our thoughts affect our speaking, our acting and our re-acting. Some parents speak before they think, some parents think too much and over analyse situations, others do not think at all!

Think about it, are your thoughts regarding your children generally positive or negative? Do you blame yourself for everything your child does or says? Do you jump to conclusions regarding your children? or just generalise every situation?

We are all guilty of thinking-errors, the trick is to have the awareness to turn that negative thinking into a positive thought, regardless of the situation. Your children will thank you for it.

Therefore, my gift to you is to consider the following statements and questions:

- Identify when the last time was that you gave your child the benefit of the doubt.
- Commit to thinking more positively.
- Think and pause before you speak to your child, particularly during times of conflict.
- Reflect on your thinking patterns.

"U" for Understanding

If you really want to create a strong relationship with your child, one of the most important things that you can do as a parent, is to understand your child's feelings and the reasons behind their behaviour. It will take time for you to recognise their unique qualities. Do you know what makes them laugh or cry, and what motivates or upsets them?

Whilst we may sometimes not understand the meaning of our child's behaviour, being curious rather than misinterpreting or jumping to conclusions can be helpful. As parents, we play a key role in our children's emotional development. So, if you want to understand your child more, try observing them whilst spending quality time with them. Be mindful of your child's environment, is it conflict free? Learn not just to hear what your child is saying but to actively listen to them, so that you not only understand your child but you 'overstand' them!

Therefore, my gift to you is to consider the following statements and questions:

- Reflect on how well you understand your child's behaviour.
- Discuss the subject of feelings with your child in an age-appropriate manner.
- Commit to actively listen to your child.
- Spend more quality time with your child.

"V" for Values

Do you have any values? Do you know what your values are? Values give us a deeper sense of self and indicate exactly what is important to us. They can change over time, but many of them tend to endure a lifetime. Most values are passed down from parent to child by our words and deeds, until our children are old enough and encouraged to begin to think for themselves.

However, if we are not sure what our values are, it is impossible to teach our children. Values can be taught from a young age, such as having a moral compass and showing consideration for others. Tell your child when you see them demonstrating one of your values, for example, saying "Thank you for helping me tidy up, that was really considerate".

Think about what is important to you: respect for others, a sense of fairness and justice, making a difference, kindness, peace, loyalty. Value your own values so your children can value their own.

Therefore, my gift to you is to consider the following statements and questions:

- Establish what your top five values are.
- Discuss these values with your child, in an age-appropriate manner.
- Ask older children which values are important to them.
- Commit to demonstrating your values in your own behaviour.

"W" for Words

How many of us have said something and then moments later regretted what we have said? You are right, all of us. Some of us go out of our way to use words that bring peace and others, choose words that have the capacity to cut like a knife.

When it comes to communication, particularly regarding parenting, it is important that we choose our words carefully before speaking. By being assertive, we can speak our truth in a calm and clear manner, particularly when our child is misbehaving. It is also important that we comment on the behaviour and not the child, to avoid crushing their fragile self-esteem.

If you do say something that you regret, consider apologising and accept that you did the best you could, and acknowledge that you are not a bad parent just because you messed up on this occasion.
In future, remember to regularly use words which praise your children; tell them how much you love them and how proud you are of them. Luckily, positive reinforcements and the feelings they inspire have the capacity to last a lifetime!

Therefore, my gift to you is to consider the following statements and questions:

- Identify when the last time was that you praised your child.
- Reflect on whether you tend to use words that are inappropriate.
- Apologise if you feel that in the past, you have been unnecessarily harsh with your words.
- Commit to using positive language with your child.

"X" for X-Factor

Is your child different? Of course, they are. Every single child is unique and is an endangered species because there is no one else on this earth like them. Every child has particular strengths and abilities that enables them to express their individuality in a social environment. In short, each child has their own X-factor!

Our job as parents, is to identify and nurture our child's uniqueness, so that as they mature, they have the confidence to play to their strengths and share their X-factor with the world. It could be that they have a patient, loving and considerate temperament. It could be that they are good at singing or playing a musical instrument, or maybe they are a natural artist, or perhaps they are academic, sporty, or good with their hands.

Whatever it is, allow your child to choose which of their special qualities they wish to develop. Remember our choice of X-factor may not be the same as theirs.

Therefore, my gift to you is to consider the following statements and questions:

- Identify what your child's special gifts are.
- Discuss with your child what their favourite pastime is.
- Praise your child for their X-factor and for just being who they are.
- Encourage your child to develop their X-factor.

"Y" for Youth

It could be said that the media have a natural bias towards reporting the negative traits of young people. Stories abound about how much the young disrespect their elders and disobey their parents, how some get involved in criminality and are a menace to society. This drip-drip effect of negative representation in the media can have an impact not only on us as parents, but also on the youth of today.

The problem is that, if society perceives young people in a negative light, how do we expect them to feel good about themselves? The answer lies with having loving parents who feel otherwise. Parents have the biggest influence on their children. Our role is to provide a supportive relationship; to give them a strong sense of belonging; to nurture their ambitions; and give them the opportunities to realise their full potential.

Society may look down on our young people from time to time, but this view does not have to be replicated in your home.

Therefore, my gift to you is to consider the following statements and questions:

- Identify how you view the youth of today generally.
- How do you view your own child?
- Recognise that you too were young once.
- Reflect on whether life for you as a young person was plain sailing or did you struggle at times?

"Z" for Zest

Would you say that you have a zest for life? Are you approaching life with a positive outlook and feeling excited, energetic; alive and stimulated, or do you find life a bit of a bind? Regardless of whether your outlook on life is positive or negative, the chances are, your children will share that view.

If they see you drift around from day to day feeling unhappy, depressed, stressed and anxious, then they may themselves feel that life has nothing to be optimistic about and replicate your negative behaviour and moods.

Fortunately, most children do not have a care in the world when they are young, so be careful not to sway their natural zest for life, just because life may have thrown you a few lemons. Take those lemons, make sweet lemonade and rejuvenate both your zest for life and that of your child's.

Therefore, my gift to you is to consider the following statements and questions:

- Identify if you still have a zest for life.
- If you are flagging, reflect on what can you do to rejuvenate your zest for life.
- Commit to looking for the positive in life, despite what life throws at you.
- Share your new zest for life by doing fun activities with your children, things that they would not have expected.

KNOWLEDGE | ENVIRONMENT | UNDERSTANDING | REFLECTION | ASSERTIVENESS | NURTURING | MONITORING |

Brilliant Parents Please Remember:

We all have it in us to strive to be a brilliant parent. To do so takes courage, consistent self-reflection, application and presence of mind. Many brilliant parents in the making, come to parenting with their own problems, which may have existed long before their children were born. If they are lucky, those issues will not have impacted their child, but if not,the damage can leave an irreversible stain on their child's personality.

Therefore, to avoid such circumstances, it is important that all brilliant parents remember:

- The first primary school your child attends is their home, therefore ensure your home environment is a peaceful happy place to be;
- You are your child's first primary school teacher, therefore remember your calm voice;
- Wherever you focus the eye of your camera, the image will enlarge - so choose your focus wisely;
- Validate your children's feelings - everyone wants to feel valued;
- Don't be afraid to tell your children, you love them, everyone wants to be loved;
- Listen to your children, everyone wants to be heard;

- Exhibit empathy, everyone wants to be connected;
- Have the confidence to give your child the essential vitamin NO when required, regardless of their age;
- You don't know what you don't know, but when you do know, you will do better; and
- You are stronger than you think you are.

And finally, back to our garden. I often think of the miracle of a tiny seed, buried under heaps of dirt in the darkness. Somehow with the right attention, that little seed finds the strength to germinate and push the dirt aside to come forth and flourish.

The problems that parents are increasingly having to face today, can feel just like the dirt - heavy, messy and very uncomfortable. However, you too, like the seed, can push through to the light by nurturing yourself, eating and drinking well, taking regular exercise, watering yourself with lots of positive self-talk and a spoonful of faith, so that you not only survive, but thrive, whilst you raise the next generation.

Printed in Great Britain
by Amazon